MASTERS OF PAINTING

EDITED BY

ERIC NEWTON

I. DIANA AND HER COMPANIONS
The Hague, Mauritshuis [$38\frac{7}{8}'' \times 41\frac{3}{8}''$]

JAN VERMEER OF DELFT

by

FRITHJOF VAN THIENEN, PH. D.
Professor at the State Academy of Arts, Amsterdam

LONGMANS, GREEN AND CO
LONDON NEW YORK TORONTO

LONGMANS, GREEN AND CO LTD
6 & 7 CLIFFORD STREET LONDON W I
ALSO AT MELBOURNE AND CAPE TOWN

LONGMANS, GREEN AND CO INC
55 FIFTH AVENUE NEW YORK 3

LONGMANS, GREEN AND CO
215 VICTORIA STREET TORONTO I

ORIENT LONGMANS LTD
BOMBAY CALCUTTA MADRAS

First published 1949

Text set in 11/13 Monotype Baskerville

Typography
H. VAN KRIMPEN

Printed in the Netherlands

JAN VERMEER OF DELFT

I

DELFT, to this day, is redolent of the past. But it is far from being a dead town, for it is full of life and bustle. In the process of time much beauty has been destroyed – perhaps more than was strictly necessary – but even to-day there are places where the atmosphere of the past has survived: a past that was, for a long time, rich and eventful and in which scenes of historic importance were enacted. Was not Delft a focal point of interest in the first phase in the long struggle for freedom from Spanish oppression? At that time Prince William of Orange, the 'father of the fatherland', the great, inspiring leader in this struggle, settled here for a few years. Here, too, it was in 1584 that he gave his life for his ideal. Later, in the so-called 'Golden Age', Delft's political role had been played out, but that did not mean that the town was deserted and forgotten. A variety of industries had been established and Delft earthenware, which was created in a large number of workshops in the seventeenth and eighteenth centuries, became famous throughout the world. Apart from the industrious craftsmen there was a class of solid, contented burghers, a small group of families in whose hands was the administration of the town. They were genteel, dignified men and women, puritanical in their black clothing and white collars, whose images are now to be found in museums and collections throughout the world.

Even if the worthy town of Delft was full of activity in the seventeenth century an atmosphere of quiet and calm prevailed, for life in those days was much more staid and peaceful. The atmosphere of the past is most conspicuous in the old towns of Holland when the bustle of the day's business has subsided and peace descends once more upon the sagging old houses, the narrow streets and the canals in which trees, houses and hump-backed bridges are reflected.

To feel the atmosphere of old Delft despite all the changes of later years, one should walk along the quiet streets, either at dawn or dusk, by the old Gothic churches, the towers of which have been there for many generations. To lean over a bridge and gaze at the reflections of trees and houses in the water enables one to feel something of the special atmosphere which the work of the artists of this town portrays.

In a certain sense it can be said that every town gave its painters their individual character. Within the framework of all the individual differences between the artists, the Delft School is characterized by harmony and peace, especially in the second half of the seventeenth century. Attempts have been made to explain the unusual character of the Delft painters by pointing to the almost 'classical' regularity of the way the town is built. These explanations are somewhat far-fetched, but it is nevertheless a fact that there are few other towns in Holland which are laid out in accordance with a system of regular,

5

straight streets, crossing each other at right angles round a spacious market square. The canals are not so rigidly straight; there are always slight bends and twists creating subtle gradations in the light which immediately transforms all else that might be considered hard and angular.

The number of works of art produced in Holland in the seventeenth century was as remarkable as the interest shown in them. People from all walks of life had paintings on their walls, but not all wanted the same type of picture. The more educated and wealthier (which included the Delft 'regents') fancied subjects which included, for example, *motifs* of ancient times and Italian landscapes sometimes adorned with arcadian or mythological figures. Similar preferences were to be found at the court of the princes. Those who did not appreciate such *motifs* possessed paintings of the landscape and people of their country, and although such paintings were also to be found in the houses of the aristocracy, they preferred, generally speaking – and especially towards the close of the century – representations of people in elegant drawing rooms in preference to pictures of ordinary people in a more sober *milieu*.

When one reads contemporary praise of the seventeenth century painters the impression is gained that the people of that time appreciated, above all, a true likeness of nature, and no mention is made of the other pictorial qualities that distinguish the work of an artist. Yet it was not the intention of the seventeenth century masters to present purely and simply reality itself. The elements had always been sifted and ordered, transmuted into something else. The composition was always considered intellectually within the canvas area, and adapted by intuition. The strengthening or weakening of local colour was accentuated, and efforts invariably made to achieve balance within a composition. These qualities were sensed – perhaps unconsciously – by a percentage of the buyers. Purchases were not made for the sake of investing money or from other pecuniary motives.

With a few exceptions, Dutch seventeenth century painters were specialists, but despite this most of them managed to preserve the quality and freshness of their work; relatively few degenerated into routine workers. It sometimes happened that a painter, for financial reasons, deviated from his habitual theme, but eventually he returned to the subjects he loved best even though the financial reward was smaller. Prices differed according to the subject. Dutch landscapes and paintings of animals did not sell for as much as seascapes or Italian landscapes. Next in price were the detailed interiors and the most profitable of all were historical paintings. Nevertheless the painter of Dutch landscapes, for example, composed in his studio the *motifs* he had sketched from life out of doors, relying on a faultless memory in which keenly observed impressions had been stored. In the process he followed – as did his colleagues who specialized in other subjects – the changes in style which occurred in the course of years. This remarkable evolution, which one could call an 'evolution of the eye', can be traced throughought the paintings of the Dutch School in the first thirty or forty years of the seventeenth century. At the beginning of the century there was great emphasis on detail in both representation and colour. The paintings tempted one, as it were, to set out on a journey of exploration in which one found the new *motifs* at first attractive and finally absorbing. The dress of the period seemed to be composed of various colourful parts, but gradually, as the need for greater unity became apparent, the parts were united in a homogeneous whole. The blending together of colours no longer impressed the onlooker by its profuseness and variety, but rather directed his attention

6

2. A GIRL ASLEEP

New York, Metropolitan Museum of Art [$34\frac{9}{16}''\times 30\frac{1}{8}''$]

to a few objects. The play of light and shadow, the texture of surface, the transformation by light of the simplest object – all this increasingly claimed the artist's attention. Fashion, too, exerted its influence. After the thirties diversity of colour was replaced by a single shade for the whole dress. The expensive embroideries, set with glittering, colourful stones prevalent in the first few years of the century gave way to the sheen of rich folds of smooth satin which responded to the ever-changing play of light.

This evolution, with variations, can be seen throughout the numerous *genres* of painting practised in Holland in the seventeenth century. There was tendency, in the thirties, even towards monochrome, and though later it was abandoned, the effect of pictorial unity remained.

If colour and profuseness of detail were characteristics sought by the early seventeenth century painters, so also was liveliness, and this lasted well into the second quarter of the century. The figures are all in action; they gesticulate, they chat and chaff. Farmers are at loggerheads, soldiers sit emptying huge glasses and brazenly paw the serving maid. Soldiers were conspicuous because the war of liberation with Spain was not to end until 1648 and although this did little to disturb the daily round, everyone spoke of the recent hostilities. The majority of paintings depicting the soldier's life portrayed his merry, care-free adventures. Towards the middle of the century, with the desire for concentration a corresponding change occurred in the choice of themes. After the boisterous, vivacious and coarse came the subdued tone, the modest gesture. The number of figures on the canvas was reduced although Jan Steen continued with his pictures of merry revels.

If there was one artist who succeeded more than others in surrounding the common-place things of everyday life with an aura of peace and poetry and who found in the simplest *motif* a source of purest beauty, it was Jan Vermeer.

II

It was in such an atmosphere of public appreciation that Jan Vermeer practised his art. Comparatively little is known about the life of this great painter, for what little information we possess is gleaned from odd documents and notes; the most authoritative, for example, is no more than an inventory of his possessions, made two and a half months after his death. It merely lists the various rooms in his house on the Oude Langendijck and describes the objects contained in them. A number of paintings are mentioned; a few are described and two painters are actually named — Carel Fabritius and Samuel van Hoogstraten — but no works by Vermeer himself are included. It is possible that they had been removed from the house between the time of his death and the taking of the inventory; soon thereafter a Haarlem art dealer named Columbier had no less than twenty-six paintings by Vermeer in his possession.

A few of the pictures mentioned in the inventory can be seen in the background of Vermeer's own paintings. In the *Allegory of the New Testament* (Metropolitan Museum, New York, plate 34), there is a *Crucifixion* in the style of the Flemish painter Jacob Jordaens which tallies with the description, 'a large painting, being Christ on the Cross'. The inventory also mentions seven ells of gilt leather, which can be found next to the *Crucifixion* in plate 34 and also hanging across the right foreground in plate 33. Other paintings which appear more than once in Vermeer's backgrounds are not mentioned in the inventory, but it is likely that at some time or other the artist did own them. *The Procuress* of Dirck van Baburen still exists and is exhibited in the Rijksmuseum in Amsterdam (it is in the background in plates 15 and 35). Where he used a painting more than once in his interiors, Vermeer was likely to change or add details. The small *Amor* attributed to Caesar van Everdingen (Vitale Bloch, *Oud Holland*, 1936) which appears in plate 16 and in the plate on the wrapper, can be seen in part, with a small mask added, in *A Girl Asleep* (plate 2). Another example of a variation introduced by Vermeer is the painting of the *Finding of Moses*, which is large in *A Lady Writing a Letter* (plate 32) but much smaller in *The Astronomer* (plate 30).

An additional indication that some objects may have been removed from the Vermeer house is the remarkable absence in the inventory of domestic articles in common use, which also makes it necessary to use a little imagination in reconstructing his surroundings. The house was very small, standing in the shadow of the great Gothic *Nieuwe Kerk*, with a studio on the first floor and two windows facing north on to the street. Here, according to the inventory, there were three easels, three palettes, paints, canvas, some bundles of prints, and odds and ends. Pictures were hung everywhere in the house, and in a large room downstairs there was part of a suit of armour and a helmet. There is a complete

3. A MAID-SERVANT POURING OUT MILK

Amsterdam, Rijksmuseum [18″ × 16⅛″]

absence from the list of the bric-à-brac which filled the studios of other artists of the period, suggesting again either that it had been removed or that Vermeer had a rather novel sense of tidiness and order.

Since the records are so meagre, a complete biography of Vermeer cannot be written. He was born and baptized in Delft in October 1632, and before reaching the age of twenty-one had married Catherina Bolenes (or Bolnes); they had eleven children. Very near his home was the Guild House of St. Luke (the Delft Painters' Guild), which he joined in 1653 and to which he paid – two and a half years later – the balance of his entrance fee of six guilders. His fortunes were apparently not so bright in those years, and the establishment of a home may have strained his resources. By the age of thirty, however, and again at thirty-eight, he held a prominent position in the Guild.

Nearly everything else known about Vermeer concerns the state of his finances. He seems to have been alternately prosperous and needy, at one moment standing bond for a friend only to find himself in debt soon afterwards. From a petition made by Catherina Bolenes after his death, it appears that he was also an art dealer, that he had made little money during the war with France in 1672, and that he had been forced to sell paintings at a loss. In 1675 he borrowed one thousand guilders, a small fortune in those days. It may be evidence of reliability and careful management, on the other hand, that in March of the same year his mother-in-law in Gouda had asked him to take charge of the administration of an inheritance, trusting him in all matters 'with full confidence'. Nine months later, at the age of forty-three, Jan Vermeer died.

Nothing is known of the circumstances attending his death, or even whether it was the result of accident or illness. His wife was left in somewhat reduced circumstances. She had a large family on her hands, and for a long time she was not able to pay the baker's bill. Eventually he accepted two paintings valued at 617 guilders: probably *A Lady Writing a Letter*, (plate 32) and *The Artist's Studio*, (plate 20). Vermeer's wife reserved the right to buy back the paintings at a later date, and from an agreement with the baker we know that she and her mother recovered *The Artist's Studio* (then called '*di schilderkonst*', the art of painting), which is today Austrian State property. There could be no greater proof of Catherina Bolenes's devotion to her husband's work. Happily, in later years, her circumstances improved.

One does not have to be trained in graphology to recognize from Vermeer's signature that his character was well balanced. It is sober, vigorous, unpretentious. The example reproduced on this page dates from 1667; below it is that of his wife, who retained her maiden name, as was the custom in those days. Vermeer's handwriting later developed more flourish, as if it were an expression of greater self-confidence and a desire for outward show. Compared with the curls and loops of his fellow-artists' signatures, however, Vermeer's is sober and expressive.

However fluctuating his financial condition might have been, Vermeer's contemporaries appear to have had a constantly high opinion of his ability. In addition to the official documents that dryly and briefly note a few circumstances of his life, there are also on record several statements by those who knew or met him.

The first of them is dated 1654, a year of catastrophe in the history of Delft. A powder magazine in the centre of the town had exploded, reducing to debris the houses in the section toward the northeast. Carel Fabritius, at the age of thirty-two and then Delft's greatest painter, had been killed while working in his studio. The book publisher Arnold Bon wrote a poem to record the event, and in the concluding lines he represented Fabritius as a phoenix perishing in the flames and Vermeer as the resurrected phoenix who would continue the work of his predecessor. Flowery metaphors of this kind were then the fashion, but it was indeed a promising tribute to a young man of twenty-two.

Nine years later, in August 1663, a Frenchman named Balthasar de Monconys travelled through Holland and recorded his experiences in his *Journal de Voyages*. He made a one-day trip from the Hague to Delft, especially to call on Vermeer at his studio; it was a disappointment to him that the artist did not have any examples of his work on hand. Monconys did see, however, a painting by Vermeer in the possession of a Delft baker – perhaps the same baker who later accepted paintings for an unpaid bill – but he could not understand why anyone should pay six hundred *livres* for a picture with only one person in it. One might deduce from the fact that Vermeer had nothing to show to Monconys that his method of work was extremely slow; on the other hand, as the Frenchman seems to have had little understanding of the painter's work it is quite possible that Vermeer politely put him off. Except for one other mention – in 1667 Dirck van Bleyswijck notes Vermeer's fame in his description of Delft – these few details are all that can be found about Vermeer in the documents of the time.

In later centuries he was nearly forgotten. A few paintings here and there were praised by someone who had come across them and liked them. Sir Joshua Reynolds, for one, mentions Vermeer's *A Maid-servant Pouring out Milk* (plate 3) among the Dutch works that impressed him most. But for the most part Vermeer's work passed for that of any of a number of painters of *genre* scenes and disappeared into obscurity. Popular interest, particularly in the nineteenth century, came to settle on paintings with a definite 'story' or 'point', and there was little enthusiasm for simple themes unrelated to an event.

Étienne Joseph Théophile Thoré, who wrote under the name William Bürger, was the first great champion of the Vermeer 'revival'. Travelling through Holland in 1842, this young Frenchman saw the *View of Delft* (plate 6) for the first time. It was a revelation to him. He was struck by its freshness, by a direct and sensitive rendering that to him was completely unconventional. It was the antithesis of all of the historical paintings, and of the mythological or allegorical scenes that were considered traditional in the first half of the nineteenth century. Thoré's reaction soon spread to others, but it is noteworthy that a Frenchman had taken the lead. There is an inner coherence and a balanced harmony of parts in Vermeer's work similar to that which can always be found in French art – in every piece of furniture and every French building, of whatever period.

From the mid-nineteenth century onwards, *genre* painting became more intimate, and the artists themselves began to appreciate the treatment of light in the old masters. As the

4. A STREET IN DELFT

Amsterdam, Rijksmuseum [$21\frac{1}{4}'' \times 17\frac{3}{8}''$]

'historical' emphasis waned and nature was treated for its own sake, Vermeer's work began to exert an influence that, up to this time, it had never possessed. It began to be recognized that he had succeeded in surrounding commonplace objects with an aura of poetry and peace, that he was an artist who saw beauty in the most simple subject. Finally, in the last decade of the century, two Dutch scholars – A. Bredius and C. Hofstede de Groot – were gradually able to reconstruct Vermeer's work by critical examination.

III

It is obvious that an artist with the extraordinary talent of Jan Vermeer went far beyond the training he received as an apprentice painter. Though he soon discarded the artificial influences that first affected him, we still have an understandable curiosity about the identity of his master and the source of his initial impressions. Attempts to solve this problem have stimulated comparisons between Vermeer's own work and the paintings, already mentioned, that are reproduced in his backgrounds.

Vermeer was, as we have said, at one time an art dealer. Where certain paintings recur in his own creations there is good reason to assume that for his business – perhaps even for his own pleasure – he would have purchased works personally attractive to him. There was the *Crucifixion*, by Jordaens, the *Amor* in the style of Caesar van Everdingen, and *The Procuress* by Baburen. Apart from the Flemish Jordaens, there would thus seem to have been at least two Dutch painters for whom Vermeer had a certain preference, both of them strongly influenced by the Italian School.

Everdingen had a classical and smooth manner of painting. His exactly-drawn, coolly-coloured figures may have interested Vermeer, though the latter, in the case of the *Amor*, probably considered only the values of light and tone. Dirck van Baburen was a painter of the Utrecht School who died in 1623, nine years before Vermeer was born. Utrecht was then comparatively isolated from the great Dutch centres, and its school of painting firmly retained its own character, built on the Italian model. Many Utrecht painters took the long journey to Italy to receive their training, where they were inevitably influenced by past and contemporary Italian masters. The best of the Utrecht artists, however, were independent enough not to imitate slavishly the Italian examples they so much admired. They knew how to adapt the newly-gained experience in form and lighting to their own use.

At the end of the sixteenth and beginning of the seventeenth centuries, there lived in Utrecht a painter named Hendrick Terbruggen. While in Italy, he had been strongly influenced by Caravaggio, the almost revolutionary artist who liked to use bold lighting off to one side in his paintings, thus creating deep contrasts of shadow. But Terbruggen had an inborn and delicate sense of colour, and he soon modified Caravaggio's teaching to his own genius. He knew how to create atmosphere, and he possessed a special talent for playing over a surface with subtle nuances of light. He emancipated himself from Caravaggio's influence and placed his figures in daylight; instead of sharp contrast, his shadows became transparent and the lighted parts radiant.

Though Terbruggen also died (in 1629) before Vermeer was born, the colour schemes of the two and the manner in which they both 'managed' light are so analogous that it

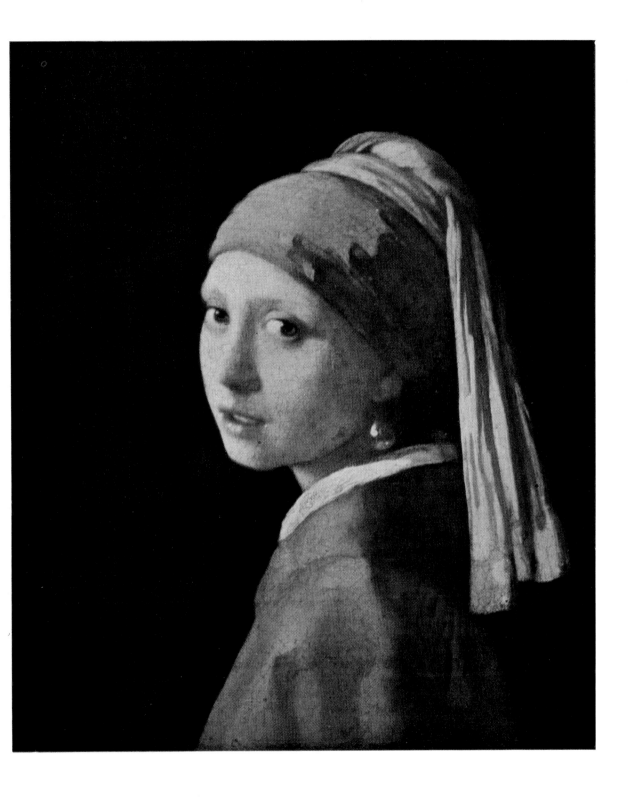

5. HEAD OF A GIRL
The Hague, Mauritshuis [$18\frac{5}{16}''\times 15\frac{3}{4}''$]

can safely be assumed that Vermeer, in his youth, was influenced by Terbruggen and other Utrecht masters. In fact, it would be tempting to deduce from this the hypothesis that Vermeer spent part of his apprenticeship in Utrecht. Unfortunately, this theory is contradicted by the very spirit of Delft that pervades Vermeer's work. It can be found preceding him in the earlier masters of Delft, like Gerard Houckgeest and Emmanuel de Witte (the latter lived in Delft from 1642 to 1652), who combined perspective studies with the play of light in the white interiors of churches.

When young Carel Fabritius came to Delft, fresh from Rembrandt's studio in Amsterdam, he too began to fall under the spell of the calm and peaceful city. Very little remains of his work, but there is enough to show that his style changed in the last four years of his life. The roughly brushed pieces of his Amsterdam period are entirely different from his last paintings, which rank among the greatest produced in the seventeenth century; *The Goldfinch* (The Hague, plate 36) and *The Guard* (Schwerin) are good examples. It is said that Fabritius was extremely fond of pictures with perspective composition, a preference shared in Delft by the church painters, by Pieter de Hooch, and at times by Vermeer.

Without arbitrarily stating that there was co-operation between the two (a theory often advanced), it can be assumed that the work of Fabritius made an impression on the young Vermeer. In such a small town they would naturally have known each other; and, through Fabritius, Vermeer would have become further acquainted with the work of the Rembrandt School, so entirely different from his own. In any case, there is good reason to believe that the character of Fabritius' work gradually imprinted itself on Vermeer's.

This influence lasted until some years after Fabritius' death. Then Vermeer slowly began to evolve a manner and a method that were entirely his own. He began to use backgrounds that were lighter than the figures in front of them. Gradually he developed his own peculiar 'grainy' technique and gradually he 'built' space around his figures.

13

IV

Compared with Vermeer's more mature work, *Christ in the House of Mary and Martha* (Edinburgh, plate 9) is very primitive indeed; it even has decided imperfections in draughts-manship. The remarkably draped folds in Christ's garment are reminiscent of the late Gothic figures whose clothes almost 'live their own lives' quite apart from the movement and attitudes of the wearers. The figures are large, placed close to each other and to the foreground; Vermeer has made no attempt to create an illusion of space. The composition follows a few broad lines: a diagonal and the two triangles in which each of the women is contained. There is a certain likeness between the attitude of Christ (the profile of the head and the extended right arm) and the Christ in a painting by Cavallino, the *Death of St. Joseph*, in Naples (Tancred Borenius, *Burlington Magazine*, 1923), but this may easily be coincidence. In spite of its awkwardness, *Christ in the House of Mary and Martha* is full of youthful promise. The painting is bold, with a facile touch, and Mary's head against the white tablecloth is a beautiful piece of observation.

It was some time before Vermeer mastered the logical and flowing arrangement of drapery. Another example of his difficulty is *Diana and her Companions*, (Mauritshuis, The Hague, plate 1). This painting is very different from *Christ in the House of Mary and Martha*, especially in mood. It has none of the clumsiness of the other painting; the construction is large, with a clear diagonal that is also the right side of an isosceles triangle, and two symmetri-cally placed verticals rising up from the sides. In this picture too, the composition is on one plane, but the warmth and radiance of colour are remarkable even though there has been some damage to the work in the course of centuries. The Diana in the centre is robed in warm yellow, the turned figure on the left is wrapped in a garment of orange-yellow, the seated nymph on the right is in red and blue, the kneeling figure in purple and brown, and the figure in the background in very dark attire. The small copper wash-bowl gleams brightly.

That certain aspects of the painting are reminiscent of the Utrecht School is less im-portant than the fact that Vermeer has succeeded in creating a strange, dreamy, lyrical atmosphere comparable only to those achieved by the Venetian, Giorgione. *Diana and her Companions* gives an impression of absolute silence; every figure is wrapped in thought. The subject, of course, would easily have lent itself to details and anecdote, yet the artist pre-ferred the lyricism of a silent company. Philip Hale has doubted the attribution of this painting to Vermeer, but the opinion is shared by comparatively few. The lighting and the mild, all-embracing shadows are admittedly absent in Vermeer's later work, and the whole piece is resolved into masses of colour, in contrast to the more minute and detailed technique that was to come. All the same, in that quiet mood something of Vermeer's spirit can be

6. VIEW OF DELFT
The Hague, Mauritshuis [38½″ × 46″]

recognized. The wide differences between *Christ in the House of Mary and Martha* and *Diana and her Companions* are best taken as an indication that the work of Vermeer's youth followed varying currents.

The third piece, *The Procuress* (formerly Dresden, plate 10), not only signed but dated 1656, is again very different. Here there is no lyrical charm; the story of beauty being sold for money is boldly presented. Again there is little indication of depth, and an unobtrusive composition of diagonals and triangles. Coolly and cynically the painted girl sits while the coarse customer counts out his money and the procuress herself looks on with greedy eyes and a wicked grin. The theme was by no means new; there were countless variations on it and the subject was treated several times by Utrecht artists, who showed a few large, half-length figures placed close together. Seldom, however, did a painter characterize the figures as strongly as Vermeer has done, especially in the shape and pose of the hands. As for colour, attention is concentrated on the girl's light bodice and the brilliant red doublet of the man; these are re-echoed in warmer tints in the colours of the Persian rug over the balustrade in the foreground. Bold brushwork – almost impressionistic – is clearly noticeable in the light areas.

The three figures are the 'actors' in the scene, but near them sits a young man with a lute (part of which can be seen projecting above the balustrade) – the musician to be called upon if desired. His face is in a shadow, as is Diana's in *Diana and her Companions*, and his costume is also dark. His glass is raised and he laughingly exchanges a knowing look with the spectator as if, at any moment, he will wink at him. It is this moralizing figure which impresses the observer with the tragi-comedy of the scene being enacted. He is nearest the foreground and therefore slightly larger than the others; he seems somewhat removed from them by the shadows and his darker colour. It might be concluded that Vermeer has used himself as a model.

Each time the author of this essay has studied the original painting he has found this impression confirmed. The whole appearance of the young man suggests the artist seeing himself in a mirror. The glass is raised with the left hand; the headgear is a beret, commonly worn by artists (note, for example, *The Artist's Studio*, plate 20). The age would also correspond, as Vermeer celebrated his twenty-fourth birthday in October 1656. To what extent can Jan Vermeer be identified with this gay youth, the 'commentator' on a common but questionable transaction? We gather that he was a quiet, balanced man, but he might well have had merry moods and depicted himself here giving good-natured comment. Humour in those days was crude, and a man without humour could not have conceived this painting; note especially the treatment of the greedy young client. In his later work Vermeer never let himself go to the extent that he has here, and as he advanced in years his paintings became calm and comfortable. Frequently his figures gaze at the onlooker, but never so directly or so eloquently as in *The Procuress*.

After Vermeer had experimented with such works as these, he gradually found his own style. Hitherto in his paintings, attention had been divided between the various figures and their colours, but now he slowly began to develop that great concentration that is one of his main traits – concentration of mood, colour, and form.

There is concentration of mood because no element distracts from the simple event, usually nothing more than the quiet companionship of a few people, or a solitary figure absorbed in reading or some simple task.

There is concentration of colour because the various hues and shades balance each other perfectly. Naturally strong colour and glittering reflections are softened to harmonize with the whole; natural dullness or subdued colour is enlivened. Everything is graded, corrected, regulated.

Finally, there is concentration of form because Vermeer preferred to render only a portion of a figure; he continually rounded off the contours. There are only two examples of his figures stretching out an arm or hand (*Christ in the House of Mary and Martha*, plate 9, and *A Young Lady with a Pearl Necklace*, plate 21). Even here there is no effect of sharp outline; the gesture is caught up and the contour closed. In the *Pearl Necklace*, the small, rounded – not pointed – hand of the young woman is reconnected with the body by the string of the necklace. Few other painters of that time have achieved concentration of form by the same technique; Gabriel Metsu and Gerard Terborch used part figures, Jan Steen rarely, and Pieter de Hooch only when he followed the example of Vermeer (the *Gold Weigher*, in the Kaiser-Friedrich Museum Collection, Berlin).

It is worth while to compare various paintings by Vermeer with the reproduction given here of Metsu's *The Letter* (Beit Collection, London, plate 37). The painting was probably inspired by Vermeer and there is a similarity in style, but the spirit is utterly different from Vermeer's. Everything is viewed in a more detached way, and there is no relation between contour and concentration. The broken outline of the servant inquisitively lifting a small curtain from a picture would be unthinkable in a Vermeer; and the small dog introduces an element of anecdote which distracts, or rather divides, attention. From the standpoint of composition, that space does need filling up, but Vermeer would not have introduced the element of tension – as if the dog might start barking at any moment.

Gradually Vermeer created space around his figures. *A Girl Asleep* (Metropolitan Museum, New York, plate 2) is the first instance in which he attempted to put a palpable distance between the foreground and the main figure of the painting. The piece of tablecloth and the arm of the chair, placed diagonally, obviously direct attention to the near foreground. The view through the open door, however, is a rather laboured device to create distance, and it was later to disappear under the influence of an increased feeling for concentration.

The building of depth can better be studied in *A Maid-servant Pouring out Milk* (Rijksmuseum, Amsterdam, plate 3), where for the first time his composition shows the use not only of a diagonal in plane (left above to right below) but also of a diagonal in depth. This gives a genuine suggestion of space, and the body of the woman is unusually plastic in representation. Here we also have the earliest example of Vermeer's typical and extremely personal *pointillé* ('dotted') technique, giving an effect of moving light. These specks of light can be found on the crumbly bread on the table and on the dress of the woman, particularly the dark blue apron. The manner in which the figure is placed against the light background, and the white of the coif against the whitewashed wall, is almost a miracle of craftsmanship.

Another of Vermeer's early masterpieces is the *Lady reading a Letter at the Open Window* (formerly Dresden Museum, plate 12). A certain amount of space is naturally created by the table which stands boldly in the foreground parallel to the canvas. Here begins the concentration of colour through harmony of green and red on which the whole composition

7. WOMAN IN BLUE, READING A LETTER

Amsterdam, Rijksmuseum [$18\frac{1}{4}'' \times 15\frac{3}{8}''$]

is based. The curtain in the foreground is green, the bodice of the young woman greenish-yellow. These are counterbalanced by the warm red of the tablecloth and the brick red of the curtain before the window. This painting also shows the crumb-like dots of paint, and the broken reflection of the girl's face in the glass is an inspiration in itself.

The *Officer with Laughing Girl* (Frick Collection, New York, plate 13) belongs to the same period; it corresponds in construction and there is similarity even in small details like the woman's bodice. Judging by the costumes, *The Music Lesson* (Buckingham Palace, plate 14) must also be placed in the years between 1656 and 1660. The problem of space appears to have pre-occupied Vermeer for some time, and the size of the table in the foreground – almost too large – might suggest that Vermeer had used a *camera obscura* in planning this painting. The figures blend admirably with the furniture to form one whole, as though they were all equal parts of a sublime still life. *The Concert* (Boston, plate 15) is similar in conception and belongs to the same period.

Vermeer next began to think in terms of extreme finesse. His early works were built with broad brush strokes; later there is a more delicate treatment. Form is clearly defined but subtly achieved, with colour against colour and tone against tone. The shadow masses, too, remain transparent. Small touches of paint are placed next to each other with great care, sometimes with almost imperceptible transitions, covered by a light glaze. He juxtaposed bright yellow and blue tints, generally with a light-coloured background of white or yellow.

After his early period, when Vermeer used red, it was usually in areas that did not catch the light. The result was an enlivening and balancing effect; see, for example, the *Young Woman with a Water Jug* (plate 8) and the hair ribbon in *A Young Lady with a Pearl Necklace* (plate 21). The primary colours in the former picture are the mild yellow of the bodice, the blue of the skirt, and the splendid white of the coif, placed with great delicacy against the differently graded white of the background. A length of blue material hangs over the arm of the chair; the gleam of the jug is toned down so as not to intrude on the harmony of the whole. The varied light and cool tints are then contrasted and held in equilibrium by the dull red of the tablecloth. Although the red offsets what would otherwise be a very cool effect, it is so modestly applied that the yellow and blue tints are dominant. That he was able to achieve this delicate balance would alone be evidence of Vermeer's genius.

V

It is not possible, within the limits of this book, to review the entire course of Vermeer's development; for that matter, the illustrations speak best for themselves. The reader should be warned, however, that whoever determines the succession of undated works should not follow too closely any rigid groupings based on subject matter. The human spirit, especially that of a creative artist, is not so easily confined within sharply divided boundaries. But there are certain guiding principles: the development of technique, the tendency toward enrichment or simplification of composition themes, and the history of dress or hair styles. These factors all help to date a picture, though when applying the last it must be remembered that styles remained fashionable longer in Delft than, for example, in the elegant court at The Hague.

There are only three dated works by Vermeer: *The Procuress*, 1656 (plate 10); *The Astronomer*, 1668 (plate 30); and *The Scholar*, 1669 (plate 31); the dates of all other paintings can only be approximated. Some idea of the method of dating used can be given by a short explanation of changes in styles during that time. After 1650 the hanging locks on both sides of the face became more slender; they were bound together and the forehead left completely free (plates 7 and 21). After 1660 there was a tendency towards breadth of coiffure, with hair on either side of the face and a few sausage curls in the form of a bun (plate 27). In 1670 profuse curls had begun to be the fashion; Vermeer shows a simplified version in the picture reproduced on the wrapper. The bonnet of the seventies was smooth, with a wide pouch at the back for the bun and two rounded folds above the forehead (plate 32). Sleeves became progressively shorter, very much so in 1670 (plate 32).

The male headdress (plates 13 and 17) hardly changed until about 1665, when it was replaced by another style – small, with a very flat crown. Men's sleeves also became shorter towards 1660, then reaching to just above the wrist and revealing some ot the shirt sleeve (plates 13 and 18). The jacket of the painter in *The Artist's Studio* (plate 20) was not worn in that style until after the early 1660's.

If we review Vermeer's works in the order thus given it can be seen how, in the years shortly after 1660, the young painter's vision became extraordinarily contemplative. His technique became more refined, his brush-stroke more delicate, and his tone nuances seem more breathed on to the canvas than brushed. Occasionally he followed his *pointillé* technique (plate 27). Of this series painted after 1660 it is the *Woman in Blue, reading a Letter* (Amsterdam, plate 7) that reaches a pinnacle of sober delicacy. Vermeer here renounced all local colour and set the piece in a key of nuances, blue against a background of yellow tints. To carry concentration to its utmost limit, even the red or pink tints of the complexion were avoided. Other works may rank with this one, notably *A Woman Weighing Pearls** (Washington, D.C., plate 23), a painting that inspired Pieter de Hooch to its remarkable counterpart, the *Gold Weigher*, in the Kaiser-Friedrich Museum in Berlin. De Hooch's work has a warm, rich colour-scheme, whereas Vermeer's is attuned to the whiteness of pearls. Note the beam of light and the atmosphere with which the room is pervaded. Similar, but even lighter in tone, is the *Pearl Necklace* (plate 21).

Vermeer's work became excessively finished and smooth toward the end of his life. It should be remembered that during this period he was poor and so may have undertaken commissions which demanded a certain 'point' in the episode depicted. Thus, the *Allegory of the New Testament* (New York, plate 34), while brilliant in detail, is on the whole a failure. *A Lady Seated at the Virginals* (National Gallery, London, plate 35) is another picture which could hardly be included among his best works. Whether or not financial troubles were really the cause of this change in Vermeer's approach to painting, the loss to the world of art is a great one. When he did not work on commission, Vermeer imposed the most strict discipline on himself in the severity and economy of his forms, even in his last works. Notice, for example, how *A Lady Standing at the Virginals*, reproduced on the wrapper, is constructed on a rigorous system of horizontal and vertical lines.

In addition to this series of half-length figures, he painted perhaps one actual full-length portrait of a woman in the black apparel of the regents; it is the *Portrait of a Woman* in Budapest (plate 19). Further, there are a few heads of girls. Of them, the *Head of a Girl* (Mauritshuis, The Hague, plate 5) is best known; it can be dated in the 1660's by the careful brush treatment and soberness of arrangement. The background is dark and the bodice, yellow with green touches, stands out against the blue and yellow of the kerchief; in the centre the full light is caught in a splendidly painted teardrop pearl. The features, treated cautiously with barely perceptible transitions, are tender; the lips are moist and slightly parted and the eyes gaze straight into those of the onlooker. There was once a similar girl's head in the Arenberg Collection in Brussels but its whereabouts has been unknown since 1914.

Young Girl with a Flute displays a free use of pointillism (Washington D.C., National Gallery, plate 26); she is wearing a striking 'Chinese' hat that might have been a studio property of Vermeer's. There are a few other heads of girls, but caution should be exercised in attributing them to Vermeer.† Attention has been drawn – most recently by A. B. de Vries – to portraits and studies of heads by Michael Sweerts which are reminiscent of Vermeer in treatment and technique.

It is conceivable that the girl in the Mauritshuis was Vermeer's daughter. While this is only conjecture, there is certainly a striking likeness to the small creature posing as a model in *The Artist's Studio* (plate 20). The latter must date from the same period, and it is among the most perfect works Vermeer ever produced. Not only is there an affinity between the heads of the two girls, but also in the treatment of their costumes; a cautious

* Although the title officially given by the National Gallery, in Washington, D.C., is *Woman Weighing Gold*, the author submits that the painting is incorrectly titled.

† Many authorities agree with the author that the two heads in the National Gallery in Washington, *The Smiling Girl* and *The Lacemaker*, are not by Vermeer. They have therefore not been included.

manner of painting is noticeable in both, and only in the tapestry can one find the freer, crumb-like touches.

Finally there are two examples of Vermeer as a painter of street scenes. *Het Straatje* (*A Street in Delft*, plate 4) can be placed between 1656 and 1660. This was approximately the same period as *A Maid-servant Pouring out Milk*, and there is a similarity in the manner in which the pavement is treated in one, and the basket on the wall in the other.

And then, of course, there is that masterpiece – the *View of Delft* (plate 6). This work cannot be compared with anything produced in that era, either by Vermeer or by any other painter. Here again Vermeer planned a wide stretch of foreground. Where other masters would have divided this space with shadows into various colour zones – an old device to create an illusion of depth – Vermeer made his own task more difficult by abandoning this practice. Yet the water, lucid and rippling, clearly lies *beyond* the sandy strip in the foreground. The background – to other painters it would have been merely a hazy distance – is partly bathed in golden sunlight, partly shadowed by clouds moving across the sky. Only the original painting quite conveys the superb manner in which the reddish brown and blue roofs are sharply edged against the light transparent sky, darkened by heavier clouds toward the top of the picture. The colour of the brick walls glows warmly and the accents of natural stone are deftly outlined. The many Dutch 'topographical' painters of that time were precise and minute in their detail, but compare the vision of Vermeer which, although perceptive to detail, never loses sight of the whole and is narrative as well as quietly contemplative.

Had he not died so young, Jan Vermeer might have extended the influence of his work to the point it reached only centuries after his death. He might have been able to usher in an entire new school of painting while he was still alive. Though he may have been indebted, as any painter is, to the influence of other masters, he passed through an inner development which raised him, a figure of solitary grandeur, head and shoulders above his contemporaries. There were great artists before Vermeer and great artists thereafter, but in his own sphere he was supreme.

8. YOUNG WOMAN WITH A WATER JUG
New York, Metropolitan Museum of Art [$17\frac{3}{8}''$ × $15\frac{3}{8}''$]

BIBLIOGRAPHY

This bibliography is not exhaustive, but a selection only of books and articles.

BREDIUS, A., *Iets over Johannes Vermeer* (De Delftsche Vermeer), Oud Holland, III, 1885, p. 217–222.

BÜRGER, W., (Etienne Joseph Théophile Thoré), *Van der Meer de Delft*, Paris, 1866.

CHANTAVOINE, JEAN, *Ver Meer de Delft*. Biographie critique, Paris, 1926.

CLAUSEN, G., *Vermeer of Delft and Modern Painting*, Charlton Lectures on Art, Oxford, 1925, p. 63–81.

DANTZIG, M. M. VAN, *Johannes Vermeer, de 'Emmausgangers' en de Critici*, Leiden, Amsterdam, 1947.

EISLER, MAX., *Alt Delft*, Amsterdam, 1923.

HALE, PHILIP L., *Jan Vermeer of Delft*, Boston, 1913.

HALE, PHILIP L., *Vermeer*. New edition completed and prepared for the press by Frederick W. Coburn and Ralph F. Hale, London, 1937.

HEPPNER, A., *Vermeer, seine künstlerische Herkunft und Ausstrahlung*, Pantheon, 1935, p. 255–265.

HOFSTEDE DE GROOT, C., *Beschreibendes und kritisches Verzeichnis der hervorragendsten holländischen Maler des XVII. Jahrhunderts*, Vol. I, p. 585–614, Esslingen-Paris, 1907.

HOFSTEDE DE GROOT, C., *Jan Vermeer van Delft en Carel Fabritius*, Amsterdam, 1907, 1913, 1930.

HUYGHE, RENÉ, *Vermeer et Proust*, L'Amour de l'Art, 1936, p. 7–15.

LANE, S., *Jan Vermeer of Delft*, London, 1925.

LUCAS, E. V., *Vermeer of Delft*, 2nd., London, 1922.

LUCAS, E. V., *Vermeer the Magical*, London, 1929.

PLIETZSCH, ED., *Vermeer van Delft*, Leipzig, 1911.

PLIETZSCH, ED., *Vermeer van Delft*, München, 1939.

THIENEN, FR. VAN, *Jan Vermeer van Delft*, Amsterdam, 1939.

TIETZE–CONRAD, E., *Die Delfter Malerschule*, Leipzig, 1923.

VOSS, HERM., *Vermeer van Delft und die Utrechter Schule*, Monatschrift für Kunstwissenschaft, V. 1912, p. 79–83.

VRIES, A. B. DE, *Jan Vermeer van Delft*, Amsterdam, 1939, 1948.

VRIES, A. B. DE, *Jan Vermeer van Delft*, London, 1948.

c 1653–1656   1. *Christ in the House of Mary and Martha*, Edinburgh, National Gallery of Scotland. Signed I. V. Meer (the first three letters run together)   Pl.   9

                  2. *Diana and her Companions*, The Hague, Mauritshuis. Has been signed but the signature is no longer visible   Pl.   1

                  3. *The Procuress*, prior to World War II in the Dresden National Picture Gallery; at present in Moscow. Signed J. V. Meer (the first three letters run together), dated 1656   Pls. 10–11

c 1656–1660   4. *A Girl Asleep*, New York, Metropolitan Museum of Art. Signed I. V. Meer (the V and M run together)   Pl.   2

                  5. *A Maid-servant Pouring out Milk*, Amsterdam, Rijksmuseum. Signed J. V. Meer (the J and M run together)   Pl.   3

                  6. *A Street in Delft*, Amsterdam, Rijksmuseum. Signed J. V. Meer   Pl.   4

                  7. *Lady Reading a Letter at the Open Window*, prior to World War II in the Dresden National Picture Gallery; at present in Moscow. There are traces of a signature   Pl.   12

                  8. *Officer with Laughing Girl*, New York, Frick Collection. Unsigned   Pl.   13

                  9. *The Music Lesson*, London, Buckingham Palace. Unsigned   Pl.   14

                 10. *The Concert*, Boston, Mass., Isabella Stewart Gardner Museum. Unsigned   Pl.   15

                 11. *Girl Interrupted at her Music*, New York, Frick Collection. Unsigned   Pl.   16

c 1660–1662   12. *View of Delft*, The Hague, Mauritshuis. Signed J. V. M. (the letters run together)   Pl.   6

                 13. *A Girl Drinking with a Gentleman*, collection of the Berlin Kaiser-Friedrich Museum. Unsigned   Pl.   17

                 14. *The Couple with the Wineglass*, collection of the Brunswick Herzog Anton-Ulrich Museum. Unsigned   Pl.   18

                 15. *Portrait of a Woman*, Budapest, Museum of Fine Arts. Unsigned. (Attributed to Vermeer but uncertain)   Pl.   19

                 16. *Head of a Girl*, The Hague, Mauritshuis. Signed J. V. Meer (J. V. M. run together)   Pl.   5

23

9. CHRIST IN THE HOUSE OF MARY AND MARTHA
Edinburgh, National Gallery of Scotland [$62\frac{1}{2}'' \times 55\frac{1}{2}''$]

10. THE PROCURESS, 1656

In the collection of the Staatliche Gemäldegalerie, Dresden [$56\frac{1}{4}''$ × $51\frac{1}{8}''$]

11. Detail from THE PROCURESS

12. LADY READING A LETTER AT THE OPEN WINDOW
In the collection of the Staatliche Gemäldegalerie, Dresden [$32\frac{5}{8}''\ \times\ 25\frac{1}{4}''$]

13. OFFICER WITH LAUGHING GIRL
New York, Frick Collection [$19\frac{7}{16}''$ × $17\frac{7}{16}''$]

14. THE MUSIC LESSON
London, Buckingham Palace [$28\frac{1}{2}'' \times 24\frac{5}{8}''$]
Reproduced by gracious permission of His Majesty the King

15. THE CONCERT
Boston, Mass., Isabella Stewart Gardner Museum [$27\frac{1}{4}'' \times 24\frac{3}{4}''$]

16. GIRL INTERRUPTED AT HER MUSIC
New York, Frick Collection [$15\frac{3}{8}'' \times 17\frac{1}{4}''$]

17. A GIRL DRINKING WITH A GENTLEMAN
In the collection of the Kaiser-Friedrich Museum, Berlin [26″ × 30″]

18. THE COUPLE WITH THE WINEGLASS
In the collection of the Herzog Anton-Ulrich Museum, Brunswick [$30\frac{3}{4}''\times26\frac{1}{2}''$]

19. PORTRAIT OF A WOMAN
Budapest, Museum of Fine Arts [$32\frac{1}{4}''\times 26''$]

20. THE ARTIST'S STUDIO
Austrian State Property [$47\frac{1}{4}'' \times 39\frac{3}{8}''$]

21. A YOUNG LADY WITH A PEARL NECKLACE
In the collection of the Kaiser-Friedrich Museum, Berlin [$21\frac{1}{2}''\times 17\frac{3}{4}''$]

22. LADY WITH A LUTE
New York, Metropolitan Museum of Art [20¼″ × 18″]

23. A WOMAN WEIGHING PEARLS

Washington, D.C., National Gallery of Art (Widener Collection) [$16\frac{3}{4}'' \times 15''$]

24. LADY WRITING
Nassau, Bahamas, Collection Lady Oakes
Courtesy M. Knoedler & Co., Inc. New York

25. THE GIRL WITH A RED HAT
Washington, D.C., National Gallery of Art (Andrew Mellon Collection) [$9\frac{1}{8}'' \times 7\frac{1}{8}''$]

26. YOUNG GIRL WITH A FLUTE
Washington, D.C., National Gallery of Art (Widener Collection) [$7\frac{7}{8}'' \times 7''$]

27. THE LACEMAKER
Paris, Louvre [9½″ × 8¼″]

28. A GIRL WITH A GUITAR
London, Iveagh Bequest, Kenwood House [$19\frac{1}{4}'' \times 16\frac{3}{8}''$]

29. MISTRESS AND MAID
New York, Frick Collection [$35\frac{1}{2}'' \times 30\frac{3}{4}''$]

30. THE ASTRONOMER, 1668
Paris, Rothschild Collection [19⅝″ × 17¾″]

31. THE SCHOLAR, 1669
Frankfort-on-Main, Städelsches Kunstinstitut [$20\frac{7}{8}'' \times 18\frac{1}{4}''$]

32. A LADY WRITING A LETTER
London National Gallery (Beit Collection) [27″ × 22⅝″]

33. THE LOVELETTER
Amsterdam, Rijksmuseum [$17\frac{3}{8}'' \times 15\frac{1}{4}''$]

34. ALLEGORY OF THE NEW TESTAMENT
New York, Metropolitan Museum of Art [45″ × 35″]

35. A LADY SEATED AT THE VIRGINALS
London, National Gallery [$19\frac{5}{8}'' \times 17\frac{3}{8}''$]

36. CAREL FABRITIUS: THE GOLDFINCH
The Hague, Mauritshuis [13¼″ × 9″]

37. GABRIEL METSU: THE LETTER
London, National Gallery (Beit Collection) [$20\frac{1}{2}'' \times 16''$]

The author gratefully acknowledges the valuable co-operation of all those who enabled him to reproduce the paintings shown in this book.

F. v. T.